LeBron JAMES

I Love Challenges!

by Michael Sandler

CONSULTANT:
Joe Jones
Head Coach, Men's Basketball, Columbia University

BEARPORT
PUBLISHING

New York, New York

Credits

Cover and Title Page, © Stu Forster/Getty Images; 4, © AP Images/Lynne Sladky; 5, © AP Images/Eric Gay; 6, © AP Images/Chuck Burton; 7, © Johnny Nunez/WireImage.com/Getty Images; 8, © Stan Rohrer/Alamy; 9, © Jonathan Daniel/Getty Images; 10, © Ed Suba Jr./MCT/Landov; 11, © Michael J. LeBrecht II/Sports Illustrated/Getty Images; 12, © AP Images/Ed Betz; 13, © Aaron Josefczyk/Reuters/Landov; 14, © John Gress/Reuters/Landov; 15, © Ed Suba Jr./MCT/Landov; 16, © Bettmann/Corbis; 17, © Bettmann/Corbis; 18, © AP Images/Susan Ragan; 19, © Marcos Brindicci/Reuters/Landov; 20, © Victor Fraile/Reuters/Landov; 21, © John A. Angelillo/Corbis; 22, © Zuma Press/Newscom; 23, © Tom Fox/Dallas Morning News/MCT/Newscom; 24, © Daiju Kitamura/AFLO SPORT/Icon SMI/Newscom; 25, © Meng Yongmin/Xinhua Press/Corbis; 26, © Jessica Rinaldi/Reuters/Landov; 27, © Daiju Kitamura/AFLO Sport/Icon SMI/Corbis; 28, © Daiju Kitamura/AFLO Sport/Icon SMI/Newscom.

Publisher: Kenn Goin
Editorial Director: Adam Siegel
Creative Director: Spencer Brinker
Photo Researcher: Omni-Photo Communications, Inc.
Original Design: Fabia Wargin

Library of Congress Cataloging-in-Publication Data

Sandler, Michael, 1965–
   Lebron James : I love challenges! / by Michael Sandler.
      p. cm. — (Defining moments : super athletes)
   Includes bibliographical references and index.
   ISBN-13: 978-1-59716-856-4 (library binding)
   ISBN-10: 1-59716-856-4 (library binding)
   1. James, LeBron—Juvenile literature. 2. Basketball players—United States—Biography—Juvenile literature. I. Title.

   GV884.J36S36 2009
   796.323092—dc22
   [B]
                                2008044341

For more information, write to Bearport Publishing Company, Inc., 101 Fifth Avenue, Suite 6R, New York, New York 10003. Printed in the United States of America.

10 9 8 7 6 5 4 3 2 1

Table of Contents

The Big Game

LeBron James had played in plenty of important games, but none more important than this one. His team, Team USA, was facing Spain at the 2008 Olympics in Beijing (*bay*-JING), China. The winner would take home the gold medal.

Winning the medal meant everything to LeBron. Before the Olympics began, he'd promised his country, "We are going to get this gold."

LeBron, looking serious, at an August 2008 Olympic team practice session

Could LeBron keep his word? Early on, things didn't look good. The Spanish team took a first quarter lead. Then LeBron picked up two quick **fouls**, and the U.S. coach pulled him from the game. For a while, LeBron was stuck on the **bench**.

LeBron blocks a shot by Spain's Pau Gasol during the first quarter of the gold medal game.

In Olympic basketball, players are allowed five fouls. After the fifth foul, they must sit out the rest of the game.

Learning to Be Tough

With the United States behind Spain in scoring, some players got nervous—but not LeBron. His mother had taught him never to be scared.

LeBron had to be tough while growing up in Akron, Ohio. His mother, Gloria James, had lots of love to give him, but little else. The family struggled to make ends meet. Often, they lived with friends and relatives.

LeBron's mom, shown here at one of his high school games, has always been her son's biggest supporter.

LeBron has no brothers or sisters and never knew his father. "My mother is my mother. But she also is my sister, my brother, my best friend, my uncle, my everything," LeBron has said. Gloria—whose name is tattooed on LeBron's arm—is the center of his life.

"My mom would always say, 'Don't get comfortable, because we may not be here long,'" LeBron remembers. "When I was five, I moved seven times in a year."

In fourth grade, LeBron moved in with the family of his friend Frank Walker, Jr. He would stay there until Gloria could find them a permanent home.

Frank Walker, Jr. (left), shown here with LeBron in 2003, has been one of LeBron's closest friends since grade school.

Basketball Dreams

Living with the Walkers brought **stability** to LeBron's life—and a fierce love for basketball. Frankie Walker's father, Frank Walker, Sr., was a coach. He taught 10-year-old LeBron the secrets of the game.

"He was better than the rest of the kids," remembers coach Walker. "But I never let him know . . . ."

LeBron lived in several houses around Akron, Ohio (shown here) before he went to live with the Walkers.

Basketball became LeBron's **passion**. "When I was in the fifth grade, I wrote down my career goals," he said. "One of them was to be in the **NBA**. My teachers would tell me I was crazy."

Yet this goal helped keep LeBron out of trouble and focused on improving his game. LeBron has said, "Basketball kept me off the streets."

Michael Jordan

LeBron's favorite player as a kid was Michael Jordan. That's why he wears number 23 today. It was Michael's number when he played for the Chicago Bulls.

King James

By the time LeBron was 15, no one was calling his NBA dreams crazy. People jammed into the gym at his school, St. Vincent–St. Mary High, just to see him play. They came from all over the country! So many people came that home games were moved to the University of Akron's arena during LeBron's final two seasons. The arena could hold 6,000 fans—a lot more than could fit into his high school gym.

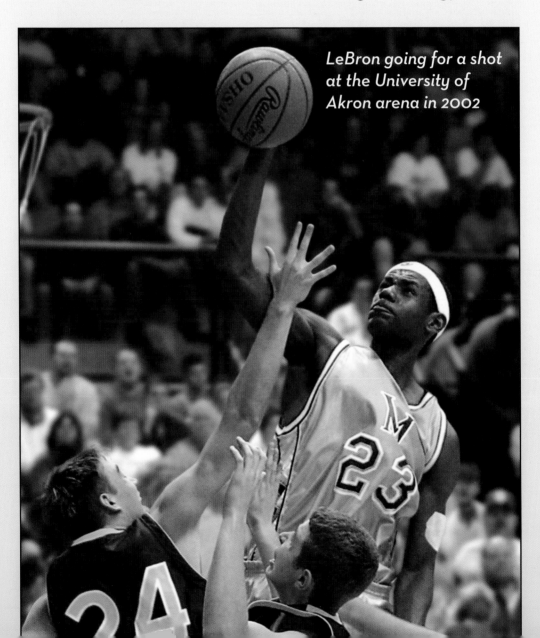

LeBron going for a shot at the University of Akron arena in 2002

LeBron led St. Vincent–St. Mary High to three state championships. By senior year, it was clear he was headed straight to the NBA. One question remained: Which lucky team would get him?

Sports Illustrated

Winter Olympics
WHAT MAKES THESE GAMES SO SPECIAL
U.S. SNOWBOARDERS RULE THE HALFPIPE

THE CHOSEN ONE

High school junior **LeBron James** would be an NBA lottery pick right now

FEBRUARY 18, 2002 www.cnnsi.com
AOL Keyword: Sports Illustrated

At age 17, LeBron's performance on the court amazed every coach who saw him play. *Sports Illustrated* magazine called him *The Chosen One*, because so many professional teams were eager to have him play for them.

The King of Cleveland

The Cleveland Cavaliers turned out to be the team. They won the top pick in the 2003 NBA **draft**—LeBron! All of Ohio celebrated.

Basketball fans across America were almost as excited as those in Ohio—and curious, too. How would LeBron do? No one doubted his basketball skills, but what about his **maturity**? LeBron was only 19. Could he handle NBA **pressure**?

LeBron, shown here being congratulated by NBA Commissioner David Stern, was the first player picked in the 2003 draft.

LeBron wasn't worried. "I'm just looking forward to the challenge," he said. "I love challenges." He soon backed up his words, taking off in the league like a rocket. With LeBron, Cleveland doubled its win total from the year before.

LeBron in his first year with the Cavaliers makes a dunk in a game against the Los Angeles Clippers.

LeBron was named **Rookie** of the Year after the 2003–2004 NBA season.

Championship Round

Each year, LeBron grew stronger. In 2004–2005, he was picked for the NBA **All-Star Game**. The following season, 2005–2006, LeBron averaged more than 30 points per game. He broke every single-season scoring record in Cavalier history. He came in second to Phoenix's Steve Nash in the MVP (Most Valuable Player) voting.

LeBron tips the ball into the basket during the first half of the 2005 All-Star game.

The 2006–2007 season was even better, though. Few people thought Cleveland had a top NBA team. No one believed they could reach the NBA **finals**.

LeBron proved them wrong. He carried his Cavaliers to their first finals appearance ever. Though Cleveland lost to the San Antonio Spurs, the basketball world was amazed.

LeBron drives past the Spurs' Tim Duncan in Game 1 of the 2006-2007 NBA Finals.

LeBron was the youngest player in NBA history to average 30 points a game.

Olympic Basketball

Only one thing can compare to winning an NBA championship—winning at the Olympics. For years, U.S. teams did nothing else. It wasn't surprising. Basketball, after all, is an American sport. It was invented in Massachusetts back in 1891.

The game **debuted** at the Olympics in 1936, in Berlin, Germany. From that time until 1968, American basketball teams did more than win every gold. They won every single Olympic game they played!

Seven members of the 1936 U.S. team that won the first gold medal in basketball

Then, in 1972 at the Olympics in Munich, Germany, the Soviet Union (today's Russia) took the gold in a **controversial** win. In 1988, at the Olympics in Seoul, South Korea, the Soviets beat the U.S. team again. In both losses, young U.S. college players faced older, more experienced Soviet players.

U.S. players after the 1972 Olympic loss to the Soviets

In 1972, the Soviet Union was given two extra chances to score the winning basket. American players felt cheated. They refused to accept their silver medals after the 51–50 loss.

Dreams and Nightmares

For the 1992 games in Barcelona, Spain, the Americans evened the playing field. Instead of college players, the United States sent NBA stars to the Olympics.

The '92 U.S. Olympic basketball team was nicknamed the Dream Team. It was a team like no other in history. With future **hall-of-famers** such as Larry Bird, Michael Jordan, Magic Johnson, Charles Barkley, and Patrick Ewing, the Dream Team easily won the gold.

The 1992 Dream Team won every game it played, winning games by as much as 60 points. Here, Michael Jordan sails high above Magic Johnson to knock away a shot.

Three Olympics later, however, the world once again caught up with the Americans. In Athens in 2004, the NBA pros lost three games and had to settle for a bronze medal. Americans were shocked. The players were crushed, especially the team's youngest member—LeBron James.

Argentina's team celebrating after winning the 2004 Olympic gold medal

LeBron was just 19 at the 2004 Olympics—only one year out of high school. He was the youngest U.S. Olympic basketball player in 35 years.

Team Leader

Though LeBron wasn't to blame for the 2004 loss, he still felt terrible. He swore to come back in 2008 and help the United States win. This time, he wouldn't be the team's young rookie. He would be Team USA's leader.

"I knew it had to come from someone," LeBron said, shown here talking with Kobe Bryant (left) during an Olympic practice game. "It doesn't matter how good individuals are, if you don't have a leader, it's not going to be right."

LeBron's new role would make a big difference. As teammate Dwyane Wade predicted, "When you watch us play this summer, you're going to be hearing LeBron on the court, yelling and screaming, talking on defense. There's going to be that leadership that we need." At every practice, LeBron urged his teammates to work harder: *"For us, it's now or never. It's the gold, or it's failure."*

The 2008 Olympic basketball team (Team USA) and coaches

Team USA 2008 Roster

Guard
#5 Jason Kidd
#7 Deron Williams
#8 Michael Redd
#9 Dwyane Wade
#10 Kobe Bryant
#13 Chris Paul

Forward
#4 Carlos Boozer
#6 Lebron James
#12 Chris Bosh
#14 Tayshaun Prince
#15 Carmelo Anthony

Center
#11 Dwight Howard

Olympics 2008

The Beijing games began, and Team USA coasted through six easy wins. Time and again, LeBron led the way. He hit from inside and outside. He passed the ball to open teammates. He scrambled for **rebounds** and dove for **loose balls**.

LeBron struggles with Australia's Joe Ingles during a preliminary game at the 2008 Olympics.

The Americans outscored their opponents by 30 points a game in their six wins.

The victories sent the team on to the **medal round**. First they faced the 2004 Olympic champions from Argentina. The U.S. team quickly broke into the lead.

Then, when Argentina tried to squirm back into the game, LeBron took over. He sank two three-pointers to build a huge lead. The United States won easily. America was headed to the gold medal game.

LeBron reacts after one of his three-point shots against Argentina.

Spanish Champions

In the final game, Team USA would play Spain, basketball's 2006 World Champions. The Spanish team was packed with NBA players, including two seven-foot-tall (2.1 m) brothers, Pau and Marc Gasol. Beating them would be Team USA's final challenge.

Pau Gasol (in white), shown here with Kobe Bryant, was an NBA All-Star player and a Los Angeles Laker.

In addition to the Gasol brothers, three players on the 2008 Spanish Olympic team had played for or signed with NBA teams—Jose Calderon with the Toronto Raptors, Rudy Fernandez with the Portland Trail Blazers, and Juan Carlos Navarro with the Memphis Grizzlies.

The Spaniards came out blazing, hitting seven of their first nine shots. Then LeBron had to leave the game with fouls. On the bench, he thought about what he had to do: *Play defense. Share the ball. Lead the way.*

When LeBron checked back into the game, everything sped up. *Slam!* He powered inside to score. *Swish!* He sank a long three-pointer. *Swat!* He **tipped** the ball from a Spaniard.

LeBron, in mid-air, dunks the ball during the 2008 gold medal game against Spain.

25

Gold!

LeBron's teammates matched his effort. Jason Kidd pressured Spanish **ball handlers**. Dwyane Wade stole the ball and dunked it. Chris Bosh and Tayshaun Prince grabbed rebounds. Kobe Bryant hit shot after shot. Team USA built a huge lead.

Dwyane Wade goes for a basket as Pau Gasol (#4) tries to block the shot.

Though Spain tried to come back, the Americans held on for a 118-107 win and the 2008 gold medal. No one was happier than the team leader. LeBron knew what it had taken to earn it.

"If it wasn't for the determination and the willpower we had, we would not have gotten this win," LeBron said. "Much respect to Spain, but the U.S. is back on top."

LeBron (center) and teammates celebrating the gold medal victory

The U.S. men's basketball team went 8-0 at the 2008 Beijing Olympics. It marked the 13th time the United States had won the gold.

Just the Facts

■ In LeBron's freshman year of high school, his basketball team finished with a perfect 27–0 record. LeBron averaged 18 points a game. In his senior year, he averaged 30 points a game.

■ In high school, LeBron also played football. He loved catching passes. He was talented enough to be named **All-State** as a wide receiver in his sophomore year.

Timeline

Here are some important events in LeBron James's life.

1999
Begins freshman year at St. Vincent-St. Mary High School

1984

1998

2000

1984
Born December 30 in Akron, Ohio

■ During the 2003–2004 NBA season, LeBron became the youngest player to score 1,000 points. During the 2007–2008 season, he became the youngest player to score 10,000 points.

■ LeBron has scored more than 50 points in an NBA game five times. His career high of 56 came against the Toronto Raptors in 2005.

■ Today, LeBron stands 6 feet, 9 inches (2.06 m) tall!

■ Lebron writes and eats with his left hand.

■ LeBron has the same birthday as golf superstar Tiger Woods.

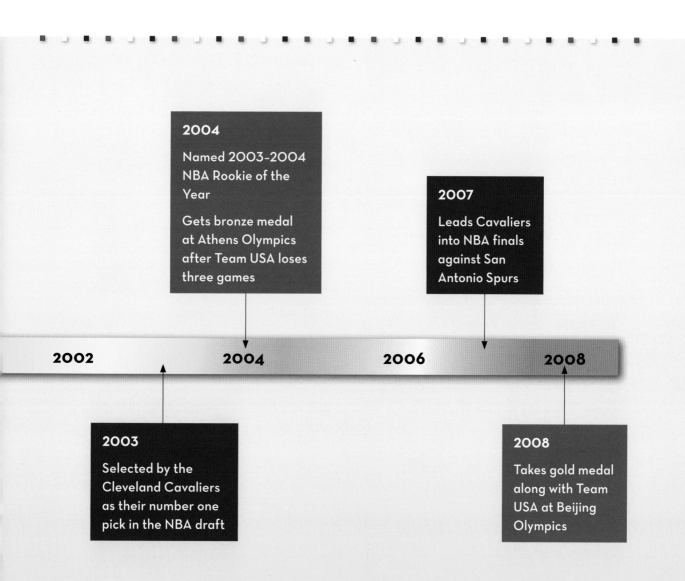

2004

Named 2003-2004 NBA Rookie of the Year

Gets bronze medal at Athens Olympics after Team USA loses three games

2007

Leads Cavaliers into NBA finals against San Antonio Spurs

2002 2004 2006 2008

2003

Selected by the Cleveland Cavaliers as their number one pick in the NBA draft

2008

Takes gold medal along with Team USA at Beijing Olympics

Glossary

All-Star Game (AWL-STAR GAME) a yearly game between the best players in the NBA's Eastern Conference and its Western Conference

All-State (AWL-STAYT) the best players in the state who are invited to play on an All-State team

ball handlers (BAHL HAND-lurz) players who dribble the ball and bring it up the court

bench (BENCH) seats on the side of the court where team members sit when they are not playing

controversial (*kon-truh-VUR-shuhl*) causing a lot of argument; not accepted by everyone

debuted (day-BYOOD) appeared for the first time

draft (DRAFT) an event in which pro teams take turns choosing college players to play for them

finals (FYE-nuhlz) the last round of the playoffs; the set of games that determines a final champion

fouls (FOWLZ) violations of the game's rules of play

hall-of-famers (HAWL-UHV-FAYM-urz) members of the best group of players ever to play a sport

loose balls (LOOS BAWLZ) balls that no player has control of

maturity (muh-CHUR-i-tee) ability to act grown-up and handle responsibility

medal round (MEHD-uhl ROWND) the final set of games that determine which teams win the gold, silver, and bronze medals

NBA (EN-BEE-AY) National Basketball Association

passion (PASH-uhn) something one strongly cares about

pressure (PRESH-ur) a feeling of worry about how one will do

rebounds (REE-bowndz) balls that are retrieved after a missed shot

rookie (RUK-ee) a first-year player

stability (stuh-BIL-i-tee) calmness and order

tipped (TIPT) got control of the ball

Bibliography

Gregory, Sean. "LeBron's Gold Guarantee." *Time*, 172:5 (August 4, 2008).

Jones, Ryan. *King James: Believe the Hype.* New York: St. Martin's Griffin (2005).

Lilly, Brandon. "It's Decisions, Decisions for LeBron James." *The New York Times* (July 12, 2002).

Pluto, Terry, and Brian Windhorst. *The Franchise: LeBron James and the Remaking of the Cleveland Cavaliers.* Cleveland, OH: Gray & Co. (2007).

Read More

Christopher, Matt. *On the Court with…LeBron James.* New York: Little Brown Young Readers (2008).

Feinstein, Stephanie. *LeBron James.* Berkeley Heights, NJ: Enslow (2008).

Hofstetter, Adam B. *Olympic Basketball.* New York: Rosen Publishing (2007).

Oxlade, Chris, and David Ballheimer. *Olympics (Eyewitness Books).* New York: DK Children (2005).

Learn More Online

To learn more about LeBron James, the NBA, and the Olympics, visit **www.bearportpublishing.com/SuperAthletes**

Index

About the Author

MICHAEL SANDLER has written numerous books on sports for kids and young adults. He lives in Brooklyn, New York, with fellow writer Sunita Apte and their two children, Laszlo and Asha.